GROUND HOG DAY

Nydia Caraman

ISBN 978-1-64468-422-1 (Paperback)
ISBN 978-1-64468-423-8 (Hardcover)
ISBN 978-1-64468-424-5 (Digital)

Copyright © 2020 Nydia Caraman
All rights reserved
First Edition

All rights reserved. No part of this publication may be reproduced, distributed, or transmitted in any form or by any means, including photocopying, recording, or other electronic or mechanical methods without the prior written permission of the publisher. For permission requests, solicit the publisher via the address below.

Covenant Books, Inc.
11661 Hwy 707
Murrells Inlet, SC 29576
www.covenantbooks.com

PREFACE

This book began years ago when I found myself lost as to how to help my son with autism. I found myself sitting on the floor in a bookstore in tears, unable to find any help. Then it hit me: I will never find a book about my son! I was determined to write one myself in hopes of helping someone else who may find themselves in a similar situation. As a mother who has very little college education, I doubted myself. Then I took a moment and thought back on our son's life and all the challenges he had and how I helped him get through them. I told myself that I know him better than anyone else. Although I read many books over the years, I only read parts pertaining to our son.

For all the help and knowledge I have gained, I first have to thank my mother for the example she set, my cousin for the introduction to autism and how different it could be. To our son, Keith, who has been and continues to be the best teacher on his life with autism. To our daughter Denyse for being my right hand through my husband's many deployments and trips, and to the man who from the beginning of our life together has always been there. To the best husband, father and friend I could ask for, you have helped me more than you know. I love you.

GROUNDHOG DAY

My groundhog day, or should I say night; I get in bed, get comfortable, grab my iPad, and read, hoping that it will make my eyes tired. After a couple of hours, my eyes finally start to burn, and I begin to nod off. This may actually happen; I may actually get some sleep! I take off my glasses, put down my iPad, readjust my adjustable bed, (which was *so* worth every penny*)*, and close my eyes… Wait, I have to go to the bathroom, I go, get back in bed, get comfortable, and close my eyes again… My dog is scratching at the door. I let him in, get back in bed, close my eyes… And it begins: thousands of thoughts, ideas, and things I need to get done, things I should have gotten done, things I wish I had done etc.

Then the flood of frustrations revolving around our son's struggle in a world that isn't ready to help him as an adult with autism begins. What I wish I could do to help our son, should do for him, had the money to do for him, fight the lack of services for adults with autism, jobs for him or the lack there of.

Since I wasn't doing anything else, I started writing. I enjoy writing; it gets things off my chest. This way, maybe it will get out of my head so I can sleep. I have to say, having an adult with autism, or Asperger's or being on the spectrum or whatever is politically correct at the moment, seems more difficult than I thought it would be. Which, by the way, is like the difference between Coke and Pepsi; one may be a little sweeter, one may have a little different taste, but in the end, it is all still soda! As I was saying, you feel like you're in another country trying to translate for your son or daughter because they need help, but no one will listen or even try to understand! It feels as though you are standing in the middle of a crowd screaming at the top of your lungs for help, but people keep walking because it is easier to ignore something they do not understand.

So you walk around with a sore throat, repeating the never written but forever repeated speech you told so many times that just rolls off your tongue so easily that it almost falls out of your mouth before you know what is happening. That is if anyone cares to listen.

"My son has autism. He is high functioning and doing very well but still has a hard time socially. Keith is very independent and can do a lot for himself. We have taught him all we can and think he is doing well. We just wish the world was ready for him and would give him an opportunity to show what he can do. Etc."

Yeah, you find yourself talking about the struggles your child is going through or has gone through and realize you lost your audience a long time ago. At this point, I just laugh at myself; those who know me will still be there listening and offering me a hug. Seriously, it is rough. If it's this rough for me, I can only imagine what it's like for our son, Keith, who is constantly being corrected to fit in to a world that doesn't even have half the manners that he does.

We, as the parents, have spent most of our child's lives researching, making calls, fighting for services, basically becoming an expert on our children and what they need and still end up disappointed trying to make things happen for them on our own!

TEN THINGS

You will get many opinions and suggestions on how or what to do for your child. You also can become overwhelmed with the amount of information you receive, but you ultimately have to make your decision on what is best for your child and family. In saying that, these are just a few things that really helped us through.

1. Labels. Accept your child, and who they are. A "label" doesn't change anything about them just because you walk into a doctor's office. They are the same kid that walked in the office and will be the same when they walk out. I must admit that I had a difficult time with "labels" at first, thinking that all the sudden he would be seen differently like, magically, people would know that something was different, but the fact of the matter was I didn't want to see him differently.

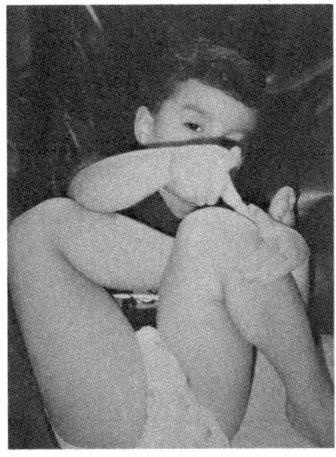

It is hard to accept at first, but I believe it's a normal reaction. I can say that now looking back. Nothing would change Keith, the way we saw him, or the way others would see him. I realize how hard it is to have a doctor tell you that something is "wrong" with your child and it has a name, but that's all it is, a name for all the things you didn't understand about your child.

Please don't take this negatively, because now you can do research to better understand your child and what he/she is going through. You will finally get some answers to the questions you've had and find ways to more effectively help your child learn. Reaching your little one is a huge gift, and the diagnosis will be just the beginning of getting there.

After Keith was diagnosed, I became a walking encyclopedia on autism; it was literally all I would talk about. I could see people getting bored with me, but I couldn't stop. It was like word vomit. One day, I listened to myself go on and on and wanted to look in the mirror and scream, "Shut up!" Talking about Keith and his diagnosis was my way of coping with the stress, emotions and acceptance.

As with anything else major in life, people will show their true colors during this time: Your true friends will forever be there to listen to you, no matter how long you ramble on. Finding out your child has a disability is a difficult process, but in order to effectively parent, we must move past the emotions and into assisting our kids as best we can.

2. Breakdown. When you initially receive your child's diagnosis or label, you may want to explode, scream, cry, hit something because you are overwhelmed with emotion; you may want to sit and reflect or blame yourself; you may want to fix it; all of which is okay. In my case, I quietly went to the doctor's bathroom and did all the above. I took it out on the bathroom stall door until I could somewhat breathe again. I didn't want to show that emotion in front of our son. I came out armed with questions, thinking it would change things, and ended up defeated.

It was something I couldn't change, something I couldn't take away or protect Keith from. It literally hurt my heart. This is all normal; let yourself feel it all so that you can move on to helping your child, because your child needs you. *But get it out, this will happen more than once, and it will not be because of your child.*

3. Research. *Do as much research as you can.* There is a lot of information out there. If you end up reading things that do not sound like it relates to your child, *stop reading it!* This will only make you worry, set you back emotionally, and waste your time. I have many books that I only read what sounded most relevant to our son. If you know your child and you have done your research, you have more confidence speaking to a doctor, teacher, therapist, or anyone who is working with your child.
4. Realization. *There is no book about your child!* I didn't realize this until our son was eleven years old. We spent so much time reading trying to find that one piece of information that would help and change everything! Well, that didn't happen, but believe it or not, life got so much easier because we had the expert in our face the whole time! *Our son, Keith!* He is our best teacher. Looking back, I had been learning from him the whole time!

I remember it like it was yesterday. I got off work and headed straight to the bookstore in search of answers for what Keith was going through at eleven years old. I found myself sitting in the aisle with the sad limited number of books, looking for something that would help me help him. After the short search, I was about to sit there and cry when an epiphany hit me like a big red truck. No one knows Keith like I do; how could I expect to find all the answers about him in any book? What was I thinking? Keith is my book with all the answers. I almost skipped out of the bookstore and headed straight to buy a big notebook and a good pin and began writing. I still have that version of the book, but it seemed I was writing from the beginning, minute by minute. It was too much.

I wrote and wrote for weeks and weeks, and one day, I just stopped. I believe it was like therapy for me because it got me through that rough patch in my life where I had a hard time knowing what to do for Keith.

Our story continues as we would watch him, see what he responds to and doesn't take well to, made note of it, and used it to help things work for him. Don't worry, it will become almost second nature to take mental notes on things that will benefit him/her.

5. Pay attention. *Let your child teach you how to reach and teach them!* This is very important! I know that some things will be much harder than others to figure out, and you may need help with but start with your child first. Always keep them in mind and the way they learn best; you will not go wrong! In the beginning, it is difficult to take in all the information because you feel so overwhelmed and frustrated. It will pass, and your focus will clear; that is when you start learning all you can to help your child.

The more you learn, the easier it will become to understand, but we all know we can't tell the future. We just do what we can.

6. Learning the hard way. I do realize that *all our children are different and have different needs, but I truly believe that ANY child can and will improve to some extent if you don't give up on them!* I know it's hard, and as stated before, you will have many stressful situations that will make you want to freak out. But your child must learn one way or another.

When Keith was about nineteen or twenty, he was in a program at a nearby college. In order to be part of this program, the young adult must learn to take the city bus for at least nine weeks. Each person had an instructor assigned to them. Keith seemed to learn the system quickly, so he didn't need the instructor for very long. Some time went by, and he was doing very well in school and on the bus until, one day, he fell asleep on the bus and missed his stop. My poor boy was told he had to get off the bus, and he didn't know where he was. At this time, I was working and accidentally left my phone in my car, but Keith was able to contact my husband, and he was able to calm him down and talk him through what to do. My husband heard a lady trying to help Keith in the background, so he spoke with her and got Keith on track. After such a stressful situation, we came to realize that Keith still had it stuck in his head not to talk to strangers, just as we told him as a child.

This was yet another eye-opening adventure for us. Not only did Keith learn from this, but we did too. The next time he fell asleep and missed his stop, he didn't panic at all; he just called, and we came to him. We learned a lot that day, and although it scares us, sometimes, learning the hard way teaches you more. The fact that Keith wouldn't ask for help because he was taught not to talk to strangers even though he needed help scared me.

7. "Getting it". *It will be rare to have your child "get" something the first time, so be ready to sound like a broken record.* They need your support and love more than anything. But when your child finally does something you have been working on without help for the first time, there is nothing more momentous! Nothing more exciting!

You want to scream this time in excitement and joy like never before, and any stress or worries completely melt away! There truly is no better feeling in the world than that moment in time!

A good example of this is when Keith went number two for the first time. He asked for the movie, *We're Back*. I told him that if he went potty, we would get it. At this time, he was five years old, and we tried everything we could think of for him to do it; I bribed him any chance I could.

I got in such a habit of saying anything that, one day, when he really wanted a movie, I told him if he went poop in the potty, I would get it for him. Denyse and Keith went to the bathroom, and he sat there while she read to him, after about fifteen minutes Denyse came running to tell me he finally did it! I ran up to the bathroom and saw the two little marbles. He did it, he finally did it at five years old! He got his movie, and we never had to worry about it again.

8. Praise. *Praise your child!* Even when it's the smallest achievement, get exaggeratedly excited so that they understand how great what they have done is; that way, they will keep doing it! Every accomplishment should have its reward. I'm not saying to go broke buying any and everything they

want; it doesn't have to be big. It could be an extra cartoon to watch before bed, extra time reading, or something simple they like but nothing big. When I did our son's visual list (which is the best thing ever for any child) I was able to think of so many little things that didn't cost anything or very little.

Think of a visual list as an appointment book. We all need or have some way to help keep us on schedule so we know what to do next; this is the same thing. For someone on the spectrum, knowing what is coming next is a huge stress reliever for everyone! Lord knows I can't remember five minutes ago; it's sad really. Our son reminds me of what I'm supposed to do sometimes and doesn't hesitate to tell me how I need to be more organized. You'll quickly learn as your child gets older that he or she doesn't pull any punches; they will tell you exactly what they think, and it's not always the sweetest thing you've ever heard.

9. Discipline. This brings me to the next point that some may have a hard time with, and that's okay, we don't have to always agree. *Discipline.* If you have really paid attention to the children/teens today, they have no respect or discipline and take no responsibility for their actions. I'm strict; I don't allow bad behavior from our son or our daughter or any other child I've taken care of.

This may seem confusing since I just talked about rewarding children. Please understand that the difference is the rewards are for things that the child needs to learn to better themselves, not rewarding a fit because they didn't get what they wanted when they wanted it. There is a big difference! I believe that all children need to learn respect, boundaries, and limits or they grow to be adults without respect for themselves or others, unable to stay focused enough to see things through or understand that everything isn't about them, so you can't always get what you want.

Anyway, in trying to teach these things, which is a lot of work but has the best reward in the end, just stay focused on the goal. I know that many people will disagree with me, and that's okay; these are just some suggestions from a mom. It helped our kids know what was expected of them, and it did help make parenting easier with less back talk and arguing. (Notice I said *less*.)

10. Consistency. This may be the hardest thing for parents at any point, but *extremely important! Be consistent.* Okay, as consistent as possible, because you don't want the kids to spot cracks in your plans and use it against you. It's us against them, and we will win! Okay, so maybe not all the time, but try!

I know that there is a lot more I could add to this list, but I'll just keep going, and hopefully, it all makes sense and, most importantly, helps in some way.

MY INTRODUCTION TO AUTISM

Everyone has their own introduction to Autism. It could have been the day your child was diagnosed, a friends' child, a show on TV, the news, a relative; no matter how you heard of it, you really don't know or understand unless it really touches you. For me, it was my cousin Manny. I first met him when I was in the tenth grade and he was about four years old. He came to live with us because of the abuse he suffered from his biological mother, who is no relation to our family. Manny was also neglected in many ways by her. She would lock him in a closet for days even as an infant, she tried to drown him with a water hose, and even left him outside in a stroller during a thunderstorm while she went into a bar to look for her next man. These are just the things I knew about. I can only imagine what he lived through in his three or four years of life with that woman.

When Manny came to our home, he didn't speak except to say mama, he still drank from a bottle, and was still in diapers. Now, all we knew about him was that he was abused and neglected by his biological mother. So we believed that he was this way because of the abuse he suffered; we didn't know what autism was at all and never even heard of it.

He seemed so different. I had been taking care of kids since I was ten years old, so I had been around kids a lot. When he became angry, he had to be put in his room but couldn't be left alone because his outbursts were violent. I remember sitting in the room with him, blocking the door, and if he came close, I would put my head on my knees and ball up to protect myself in case he decided to hit me.

Watching him, he would scream and scream, hitting himself repeatedly on his thighs, his head, his face. The bruises would show on his pale skin the next day; it was so hard to watch such a thing. I found myself crying, not understanding why such a young child would hurt this much and cause so much pain to himself. Looking into his beautiful clear blue eyes, they seem to be full of pain that he couldn't express; it seemed as though he was in a body he couldn't control.

During these episodes, he heard nothing, so we would just wait until Manny calmed down to try to speak to him. Eventually, he would calm to a soft sob that would last a while, but as he grew and gained more language, he would apologize over and over again. He would be so upset for whatever it was he did, and sometimes, that was equally as hard to watch, because when he cried, it was like he was still a small child, and it's still true today. He didn't want anyone to be upset with him.

As Manny got into his teens, he began to hit people and throw things; he even threw a TV on the floor more than once. My father had to anchor the Christmas tree to the wall for years because he would throw the tree to the floor if he got frustrated. Even to this day, it's unknown what sets him off, but it always ends with him saying that he was sorry repeatedly until exhaustion takes him over and he falls asleep.

This caused me to dislike his biological mother more for what she did to him. It was later that the word "autism" was used, not that it helped us understand him much better; it was the eighties, so not much was known or talked about at that time. As time passed, our family just did the best they knew how. The problem was as he got older and more attached to my mother, the more she felt the need to always be there, which wasn't good for either of them.

He became dependent on her, and because of that, she couldn't leave the house when school was out. If she did, he would get violent.

Needless to say, for a doctor to say the word *autism* to describe our son was terrifying for me, because I thought Keith would turn into Manny, which was still hard to believe, because I knew Keith, and it wasn't or couldn't be what he had! Please understand, it just scared me to think that Keith could be like him. I grew to really care for Manny and love him very much. I just didn't want that for our son. But this was all I knew about autism.

Of course, after immersing myself into as much information as I could find about autism, I came to find that there are different levels. I will say that some of what I read was misleading, and then I realized that not all those with autism were either like Keith, Manny, or like Rain Man. It took a long while for me to fully grasp Keith and who he was within autism and how different it could be.

To be clear, I know that there are many families that have a child like Manny, and I mean no harm because, honestly, I think it's because of him that I was a better mother for Keith. I understood more than I ever could reading a book. He taught me so much that I can't put into words. He is doing so well now. He lives in a home, works, goes on trips, and visits my parents often.

THE SIGNS

Although Keith was born in North Carolina, he spent the first three years of his life in Germany. The army moved us when he was about seven months old, and our daughter, Denyse, was three and a half. It was strange being in a different country for the first time; there was a lot to get used to, but it was a beautiful place.

By this time, I wasn't too concerned with Keith's development, but every time we went to the doctor, they said he was developing normally; he was just a big baby. Slowly but surely, things started to catch my attention, but I couldn't quite put my finger on it, just something was different. But every time we asked the doctors about our concerns, they blew it off as "He's just a boy, they learn slow" or "He's a second child its normal."

GROUND HOG DAY

As much as I wanted to believe it, I knew that something wasn't right. It wasn't until the time came when he was supposed to start talking that it really started to worry me. It was very hard to get his attention, he lined up his cars perfectly straight and had a fit if one was knocked out of place, he also separated the colors of his Legos. He also seemed to have his own language. There were many things that were obvious if you knew what to look for, but I didn't.

I was worried that he couldn't hear or what he heard wasn't clear, so I used to try my own "hearing test," and I knew he could hear, but why was he not talking, and why was it so hard to get his attention? Questions that kept going unanswered by the doctors. Our adorable boy was affectionate, play-fought with his daddy, and did things that made me question my concerns at times.

The lack of words coming from him really began worrying me between two and three. I read to my kids and played with them all the time because I didn't work and stayed with them at home. I mean, Denyse was reading at four years old and couldn't wait to go to school, so what was going on with Keith?

We left Germany when Keith was three and a half and he had a few words on board but not nearly what he should have. One of my sisters suggested that I get him tested at our new station in Seattle. When we got there, we had to live temporarily in a very small two-bedroom apartment. We didn't have many things but still couldn't unpack all our stuff because there was no space, so we stored boxes everywhere. Our room was like a storage room with a bed in it. Anyway, days after moving in, my husband had to go away for two months, so here I was in a new place and didn't know anyone.

One morning, I couldn't find Keith! I was freaking out looking around the apartment between the boxes in every room. I was losing my mind, and then I found him. He was not in his bed but under it in a small corner that wasn't stuffed with boxes. Of course, looking back, it was the move that got to him.

I just didn't know; I was so shaken up I just held him and cried. What could make him want to hide like this? What was wrong with my baby? Well, shortly after my husband left, I asked a teacher at my daughter's school how I could get my son tested, because I thought it was his hearing. She gave me the information, I called, and had an appointment for the next week. I had to know what was going on with our son.

The day of the testing came. I was only a little nervous. I drove up to the building slowly with Keith in the back seat. After parking, I took a deep breath, closed my eyes, and released it. After saying a little prayer, I turned to look at my boy's sweet face and thought, *Everything will be fine.*

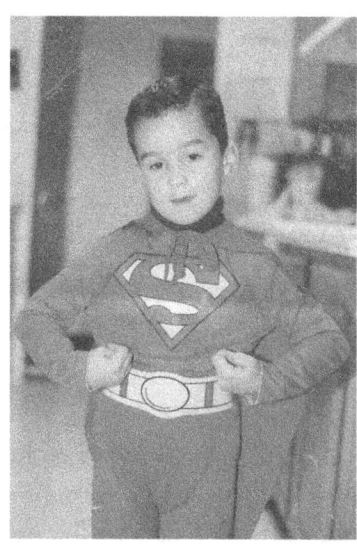

As we walked into the door, there was a lady sitting at a desk asking our name, and after telling her, we were told to sit in these old chairs. As we waited, I looked around at this old building, and it seemed very unorganized and messy, with piles of books and papers everywhere. I began to wonder if this was the right place or thing to do. I began to get more and more nervous.

Then suddenly, the lady at the desk called Keith's name. I almost froze. The lady than explained to us how to navigate the testing, because it was like a maze of hallways and rooms where he would be called in to perform tasks. I will never forget the first task was for him to simply go up four stairs and come back down. Seemed easy, except they said that he should do it as an adult would, not one foot at a time. It was at that moment that I knew this was going to get harder by the minute.

As we went from room to room, I became more and more upset but refused to let it out in front of Keith. By the end, I could barely hold it together. They called him into the last room, and he sat at a desk that had marbles in one jar and another jar that was empty. The lady asked him to put the marbles from one jar into the other jar. Keith just put his hand in the jar with the marbles and played with them.

The lady said, "No, Keith, I want you to put the marbles in the other jar." Keith didn't understand what she was asking.

I wanted everyone to leave him alone, but I knew from the beginning that this wasn't his hearing; it was much more. They took him through all types of testing, simple things that he should be able to do but couldn't. My heart literally hurt. What was wrong with my boy? Why? I wanted to scream and fall apart, but I couldn't. I felt so helpless and alone. After the testing, they told me it would be a week or so to have the results mailed to me. My jaw dropped. A week or so? You can't be serious. But there was nothing I could do.

When the package did come, it was a stack of papers that scared me all over again. I read every line at least three or four times and cried hard and long. I kept holding Keith and apologizing to him. I couldn't wait to talk to my husband that night, and he couldn't wait to get some answers as well.

The answer at the time was "developmentally delayed," and my little three-and-a-half-year-old boy started school shortly after that.

Six months later, we moved from that apartment to live on Ft. Lewis, where he went to a new school and where he had the best teacher ever, a big teddy bear of a man with a heart of gold. Not only was he a great teacher, he also listened to the parents' concerns and really cared enough to give advice. It helps to have someone like that working with you and your child.

Keith went to many different schools, and not every teacher was great, but most of them really tried to help him as much as they could. Only one teacher couldn't handle him, but she was also a new teacher all together. The school changed his class, and Keith blossomed over the year into a good student and continued to throughout his school years.

When talking about school for a child with autism, it can be a tremendous thing to think about because of the Individualized Education Program or IEP meetings. It is so overwhelming for any parent to walk into a room full of people who are prepared to discuss your child on a level different than what you have in mind. You sit there unsure and feeling unprepared. Many people don't know (like me) that you can bring in an advocate to help you through the process or do as much research as you can to be as prepared as you can. Still, talking about your child is emotional, and it can make it hard to stay focused. I knew I would be drained after discussing all that my son can't do and should be working on. I don't know if the therapist, teachers, and others in the meeting really take the time to realize that these meetings tend to be negative. I realize that it is about helping him progress, but it was draining for me.

Just know that you and your child have rights, and if you need to fight for them you can. Keep in mind your goals for your child, write them down, and keep a notebook for your IEPs to keep you on track of what was discussed and/promised. Also, you can call a meeting at any time you feel things aren't going well.

It was here that I learned the most about autism and the range of it all because I read everything I could find. This was my initial education until I realized that Keith was teaching me more than the books after a while.

FINDING OUT

At first, the shock of that moment in the doctor's office was unbearable, painful, and terrifying! When Keith ran into my arms, I wanted to take all of this away from him. It took a while, but I had to learn that he wasn't hurting, I was. Keith has always had a strength in him. Some would say he is just unaware. Call it what you will, but I would much rather see the world through his eyes.

After that, we moved to Fort Belvoir, Virginia, where we were lucky to have a great neuropsychologist reevaluate him because the schools needed a more specific diagnosis. More testing.

This testing was different. It was at the doctor's office that was well known for his work. We were told to bring Keith a lunch because we would be there for four hours or so. This time, my husband was with me, which I was extremely grateful for. As we walked into the office, we looked around and was impressed at how comfortable the room was, with couches and big soft chairs. We walked up to the lady at the desk and were greeted nicely. She told us that the doctor would be with us shortly.

At this time, Keith was almost six years old, and I was a nervous wreck. There was a set of double doors behind the reception desk that suddenly opened, and a smiling, tall man came out to greet us. He explained how the testing would go and that we had to stay in the waiting area. This scared me. I didn't want Keith to have to go through this alone. But he reassured me that he would be fine.

The doctor took Keith and invited him into his office, and that was it; I was helpless. After about an hour, my husband offered to go get something to eat. While he was gone, I could hear the doctor through the door, which pulled me in like a magnet until I was at the door. I was sitting by the door, listening to the doctor asking Keith questions and our son getting so frustrated. I was in tears when my husband returned.

My husband and I both sat there listening to our son struggle to answer questions as the doctor repeated himself over and over. "Keith, put your hands down. Look at me. What color is the sun?" Over and over. I started to cry as my husband held me together. The questions would change, but Keith didn't seem to understand what the doctor wanted, and he would answer the question with a word that had nothing to do with the question. It was extremely difficult to hear our baby getting so frustrated, and we couldn't do anything about it. A short time later, my husband was able to get me away from the door so we couldn't torture ourselves anymore.

After what seemed like forever, the door opened. Keith ran to me and grabbed my legs, and as he did, the doctor said that he is classically autistic, as if it was as plain as day. I looked at my husband, knowing I was about to explode; he took Keith, and I ran to the bathroom to let it all out. I held nothing back. Actually, I don't quite remember getting to the bathroom, but once I got there, I think I blacked out for a moment, because the next thing I knew, I was hitting the stall door and screaming. I felt like I was falling apart. Finally, I leaned against the wall and sank to the floor with my head in my hands, realizing I had to go back out there. I took a deep breath, cleaned my face, and marched back out with my chin up, ready for whatever else the doctor had to say. I tried to question him as if I knew better than a neuropsychologist, but I failed miserably.

The drive home was quiet and somber, neither of us knowing what to say to comfort each other. Occasionally looking at each other with tears in our eyes, scared of what the future held. Of course, Keith was just his regular happy self in the back seat, oblivious to our overwhelming since of uncertainty and pain.

Know that you are not alone in this and that it always gets better in time. Take joy in the goals met and look forward to the goals ahead. Believe that your child can do it and know that you can too.

GUILT AND BLAME

It is extremely difficult to have a doctor tell you that something is "wrong" with your child. No matter the circumstances, but isn't it a parents' duty to care and love that child through whatever it may be? Whether it is autism, Down syndrome, or something that could happen later in life because of an accident. Shouldn't that unconditional parental love be there no matter what? When something does not go as planed, we want someone to blame, we want something tangible that we can say without a doubt it's because of "_____" that my child is struggling!

It would feel so much better to be able to see or control what is happening, but the reality is we can't. Even if there is something to blame, what good would it do for us now? We still wouldn't be able to change anything. I believe our son was born with autism, truly without a doubt, but I wanted to put the blame on myself instead for years.

After some time past, I realized blaming myself or anything else was a huge waste of energy. I should have been spending that time on my son and what I could do for him. It is an extremely difficult thing to go through because we think that we should be able to protect our children from everything, and this proves to us that we can't, and it hurts beyond all reason. The sooner we get past the blaming, the sooner we can focus our attention on what's important—that the child is sitting in front of you waiting for your attention. Maybe someday, they will find out what the real cause is without question, but until then, it doesn't change what needs to get done today.

COMPENSATING

As parents, we do not always know when we are or that we are compensating for our child. This is not only the case for those with children on the spectrum but any parent. We do this to protect our children or not to see them struggle. Many times, we do not even realize we are doing it until someone points it out or we catch our child able to do something that we have been doing for them. When Keith was little, a doctor pointed out that we needed to stop speaking for him and have him attempt to say things that he wanted. This was the first time I realized what I was doing. I knew that by doing this, I wasn't helping at all. How could he learn if he didn't have to do anything?

I was glad to see this early on so that Keith could learn so much more, but it was difficult at first to watch him struggle. It was the best thing I could have learned for his sake. I learned how much more he could do when he started going to school as well. I must have been overcompensating for him, because I felt somehow responsible. As if I was trying to make up for something. Feeling sorry for someone doesn't help anyone. In the long run, that person may use whatever is/was wrong as a crutch to do less. We must keep in mind that most of what we teach or do not teach our kids sticks with them and will make change more difficult. Try to teach them to do for themselves as much as you can within the child's ability, and you will both benefit.

PARENTING OUT OF GUILT OR FEELING SORRY FOR YOUR CHILD

I can only imagine what it was like for our parents after raising twelve of their own kids and then bringing Manny into our family.

My mother really carried the burden of his abuse even though she did nothing but love him. She would cry for the abuse he suffered and the struggles he was having. After raising twelve children strictly, her heart melted for him. She couldn't get the thought out of her head that someone could abuse a child in this way. I think that my mother blamed his biological mother for all Manny's struggles in the sense that she saw the abuse and not autism, so it changed the way she parented him. She catered to him and was afraid of upsetting him because when he got upset, it was hard on everyone. Though our family didn't really know what upset him, they controlled what they could and not let the little stuff be the problem.

At this point, there just wasn't that much help or information on autism, so my mother did what she knew to do and showed him what it was to be loved and cared for. The thing was she unknowingly created such a solid routine for so long that he became too dependent on her and the routine. It became a situation where my mother couldn't leave the house if he was home; she could only go somewhere if Manny was at school. If she tried to go somewhere when he was home, he would have a fit. We used to joke that the "warden" was home, so Mom couldn't go anywhere.

After years of this, the stress started to show. Everyone in the family would try to get Mom to get out of the house whether he was home or not, but she wouldn't go. As Manny got older, bigger, and stronger, my parents also grew older and unable to deal with his outbursts. With the family as big as it is, someone was there most of the time, but not all the time. At this point, when he got angry, he began to go after the person he loved the most, Mom. We love Manny very much, but no one is going to hit Mom. You must understand that our mother is the true matriarch of the family. The whole family has her on a pedestal and would do anything for her. All of her children are very affectionate with her, even Manny is always kissing her and smelling her hair, telling her he loves her. He also likes to "play" with words in Spanish and English (my parents are from Puerto Rico).

Because he followed what became his schedule, it also became my mother's schedule. He ate the same thing every day; she took him a bath every night and gave him chocolate milk during his bath. She put on his adult diaper and made sure the plastic was on the bed, and every day, at about 3:00 a.m., Manny would wake her up because he wet the bed. She would get up, take him a bath, strip his bed, put his sheets to wash, make his bed, and put him back to bed. He could go to the bathroom by himself, but because it was the routine, no one knew any different, and Mom just thought this was his life, so she adjusted to him.

When Manny was about seventeen years old, a very sad day came. After years of violent outbursts, my mother took to hiding in her room when he was in a fit to protect herself from him. He was having another fit about something, and Mom was in her room while my father tried to hold him to control him yet again. This was no way to live. My parents decided they could take it no longer and called the police to come and take him to a facility where he could get help. My parents realized that it was more than they could handle.

This truly broke my mothers' heart. She felt that she failed him even though she knew it was better for them both. The police came and handcuffed Manny, who didn't understand what was happening. He cried so much, telling Mom that he was sorry, begging her with his apologies, "Please, Mommy, I'm sorry!"

Thinking back on his violent outbursts, it's as though he's like "the Hulk," because when anger took hold of him, he couldn't control himself, and afterwards, he would be so remorseful for whatever he did but couldn't control.

The facility that Manny went to kept in touch with my parents as to how he was doing and what was planned for him. After a couple months, when Mom could think more clearly, she called to see how he was doing and if he was still wetting the bed at night. They told her that he has never wet the bed since he has been there. My mother couldn't believe that, after all these years of 3:00 a.m. baths and sheet washing, he could control himself and not wet the bed. It just became a routine they both followed.

Manny is now on meds to regulate his behavior that are really helping him control himself and living in a house with a few other adults with disabilities. There are nurses and aids who help them with meds and caring for themselves. He does get to visit our parents often, but the people that work with him come to pick him up from their house in case he throws a fit about leaving Mom. Sometimes he gets upset about leaving, but most of the time, he behaves, but he always asks to stay longer and when he can come back. Every time it is close to time for him to leave, he tells Mom that he loves her house and wants to stay with her. He doesn't understand why he can't live with them again, and it would be hard to try and explain it to him in a way that he would understand.

This is not to say that he hasn't had fits since moving out or tried running away to get to my parents' house. Once, Mom had a black eye to prove it. It has been a long time since he has had an outburst because he is much better. He is in his mid-thirties and has had to move a few times over the years, but he is doing well, and he is loved very much. I am personally thankful for the knowledge he gave me. He gave me a class in something I didn't know I would be a part of; you don't always know where your lesson will come from in life, so pay attention.

SIBLINGS

When you have a child with disabilities and other children without, it can make things very difficult, and it may make you feel pulled in different directions. Giving the other child/children the attention they need can become very limited. Throughout our children growing up, I tried very hard to let my daughter, Denyse, know how important she is. I also grew up with a sister that needed a lot of extra attention and wanted to make sure that my daughter knew that she was just as significant as her brother.

The relationship between Denyse and Keith was different from the beginning. When Keith was a toddler and tried to communicate, it was like he had his own language. This went on for a long time, but the crazy thing was, Denyse understood him when no one else did. She is two and a half years older than Keith, and they had that bond that was awesome to witness. Unlike what most people think about those with autism, Keith has always been affectionate; he would hug and kiss his sister all the time. They even slept together for a while. I know that there are many with autism that don't do well with affection, but Keith will give a hug and kiss, but the hug will only last but so long. He is most affectionate with me now, and I don't mind! (He is a proud mama's boy!) I like to tease him sometimes and not let him out of the hug. He always tells me that I can let go now and we play on for a few minutes.

But back to our kid's relationship. We continually made efforts to do things just with and for her throughout her growing up. Denyse played softball most of her school years, and we went to all her games and practices. I would routinely have conversations with her about Keith and why things are the way they are. Just like any kid, sometimes she was understanding, and sometimes she wasn't, but in the end, she loves her brother and was like a second mother to him. She was very protective of him with children that came over to play with her. Some kids questioned her about Keith, and if they had a remark about him, Denyse had no problem telling them about themselves and once told a girl to go home. This is a difficult situation for any child to have such an understanding of someone who is different that they care for and how people may see him or not understand.

As I said before, Denyse even helped in potty-training Keith. Though Keith had been potty-trained since about three, he would not go number two. I refused to buy any more pampers after that. It became obvious that he would go at about the same time every day and had taken to hiding when he had to poop. I never could catch him in time.

One time, he scared me to death. We were at a store that was attached to the mall, and we saw someone we knew, so we began talking to them. Keith was not one to wander away from us, so once I looked down and realized the he wasn't next to us, I tried not to panic. I called out to him with no response. We looked around where we were standing and didn't see him anywhere. We continued to call out to him with no answer. I really started to panic and ran through the store looking everywhere, but nothing. The people who worked there started to help us and told me to stand at the entrance/exit of the store in case someone tried to walk out with him. I stood there with Denyse in my grip, crying uncontrollably. My husband searched all around the store with employees to no avail. He even went out into the mall looking for him and nothing. After about twenty minutes of hell, we went back to where we were standing and called him again, and he came out from under a rack of clothes with a huge load of poop in his pants. He was even smiling a little. I grabbed him and squeezed him in my arms, crying. I picked up a pack of wipes and took him to the bathroom to clean him up while my husband bought him a new outfit to wear. As I was cleaning him up, I was still crying; I couldn't stop. Keith began wiping my face and asking me to stop crying. He really doesn't like me to be upset. So I told him to never do that again, that he scared me and Daddy a lot, we thought someone took him, and he said he wouldn't do it again. Everything was fine because we found him, but I was a mess the rest of the day and made sure to keep letting Keith know that he can't do anything like that again.

At home that night, even Denyse talked to Keith about staying close when in public. Though I didn't ask for as much help as she continued to give, I was proud of her more than I can say. She stepped up in many ways and often, but she loves her brother, and I couldn't ask for more than that.

Always make efforts to talk to, spend time with, and play with any other children you have. Although it is hard to spread yourself out evenly, the smallest things can make a difference, such as reading to them alone in their room before bed or taking them with you for small shopping trips. Little things can make a difference. Remember that your children need you more than material things.

At times, we still have to tell Keith things that we have been saying since he was little. But know that wherever your child is now will improve if you help them learn to be as independent as possible. It will also take stress off you as the parent knowing they can do most of the self-care themselves. The true joy of the moment they master a task words can't be described! Many times, you can't gauge when it will happen, but when it does, nothing else matters; all the struggling, stress, and tears that built up to that moment in time all melt away to just pure happiness! Tears of joy and pride fill you, and you realize that, though it will take time and work, many things are possible.

LIFE

From an early age, it is hard not to notice the effect life has on our children. Our son still, in his mid-twenties, has to have full discussions about who, how, where, and why no matter how small the change. Let's face it, sometimes, we just don't feel like talking at that moment, but you have to or the questions won't stop.

But honestly, I am so proud that we can have those conversations as adults now. He has grown so much; he makes us very happy and proud! Even though some of the conversations are difficult because they are about life, finances, work, jobs, or dreams, I couldn't be happier about the fact that we can have these talks. When Keith was little, we didn't know how much he would grow and change; it's amazing the amount of work he has done to get where he is.

Did I mention that he is amazing? As I am writing this, I realize how far he has come and how far we have come as a family. From knowing nothing about autism to writing this book, raising money every April, and donating to a great cause and really wanting to help others.

We still don't have all the answers but who really does?

We all know that life is hard sometimes, but when you have an adult with a disability, it's even more difficult because you must really depend on others' kindness and understanding. You may feel as though you've lost control, control of what happens to the adult you now have with new challenges, and you miss the security the schools gave you. That feeling of comfort knowing you could fight for what was needed and have school support. Now what? What does his future look like? Will anyone hire him/her, and will the employer keep him on?

For Keith, it has been a long hard road, and he is still young. He's been fired and laid off, and it has taken years to get these opportunities! There is the VR (vocational rehabilitation) program every state has in order to help those with disabilities find jobs, but it definitely needs to be improved and have better, more caring people to work with!

It is understandable that this could be a hard and stressful job, and let me be clearer, VR finds organizations that work with Keith to find jobs. They don't do it themselves. But we have been through enough to know that it's hard to find understanding nice people for these positions. The one person we liked no longer works for VR.

The way it works is once the person finds a job and keeps it for a certain period, their case is considered closed because they have found employment that works for them. This I can understand to a point. There was a time that Keith had a job for a year and was laid off; we had to reapply and start all over. If Keith had been fired, they would have continued with his case right away.

This sounds like a system that should work, but because of all that we have been through with the poor services he received last time, it stinks to think that we should start all over again! I should say that I was applying to jobs nonstop since he got this job, so to think that he will be without a job, there will be more pressure to find him new employment.

Nevertheless, he got through it! We spoke with him a lot about how important he is, not just to us but as a person, and the difference he can make in how people see those with autism.

We pray every day that things will change, and the world will at least be more understanding of those with special needs. When I see all the protesting and/or arguing about those wanting more rights or understanding for this or that, I think, what about Keith? What about the fact that more than 90 percent of adults with autism or on the spectrum are unemployed?

Yes, there are laws in place for there to be no discrimination against people with disabilities, The Americans with Disabilities Act, to gain employment. Though I am grateful for this act and know that many of those with disabilities are able to find and keep employment, let's be realistic with the way most companies have someone apply for jobs. Online, it is keeping those with developmental disabilities from shining enough to even get an interview. I have a hard time filling out those applications because they are asking social situational questions and are looking for specific answers. This way, they weed out those that don't "fit" before given a chance.

Keith understands more than we know, and so does your child/adult. Sometimes, it feels like an uphill battle, but I will never give up on him because he deserves the best! He has such a good heart and is the best person I know, so I will keep on talking, digging, and begging if I have to in order to get him what he deserves, even if it takes the rest of my life!

Keith has gone to classes to help him be independent, learn job skills, and how to care for himself! We have spent his whole life trying to help him be as independent as possible, teaching him how to cook, clean, self-care, have manners, and yet at times, it seems as though it is not enough! I have always taken pride in being a mother! It's the best job in the world! I tried so hard, thinking that if I did my part in teaching him as much as I could, it would make his adult life easier. I know that it really has made a difference, but I guess I want it all for him. I want him to be able to have a job that he enjoys and be happy. I realize that most people do not like their jobs but go to work every day because it's life, and until the dream job comes along, this is what it is. I'm asking a lot, I know, but I'm a mom and want the same for our daughter; the difference is she can understand it all and Keith has a difficult time understanding how life works. Life is teaching us all a lesson. He has to learn about life, and I guess it is a good thing, because I want him to have a life like everyone else.

REALITY

For my husband, the hardest part of Keith having autism was the day of his diagnosis. For me, adulthood is by far the most frustrating part of his life to date! Having to depend on other people to help him is extremely difficult. When he was younger, I could figure things out to help him. True, some things took longer, but he would always get it. Now, as an adult, he is and wants to be more independent. Trying to teach him all the things of life can become a constant conversation, especially when he has the attitude that he knows everything. I shake my head, a teenager still… I know that he will get these things eventually though.

People who know our family, and especially Keith, know how great he is and how hard we have worked to help him get where he is. It's just so unfair that not just our son but many others in his situation can't do much to change anything about the systems in place for adults with autism.

GROUND HOG DAY

Frustrating is putting it lightly. There are programs out there that would be perfect and would teach him everything he needs to learn in life that we cannot. They are popping up everywhere, only who can afford almost thirty to forty thousand a semester? Oh, and there isn't financial aid available, because it is a non-degree program! So let me just pull out my checkbook and take care of that... If I could afford that, he would have gone a long time ago!

Our son deserves better than what is offered by the state, government, whomever is in control of this situation! So I ask this question. After all this schooling, therapy, training, life skills, time, and money spent on all that is offered during school age, what good does it do if, at the end of the day, autistic adults are still sitting in their rooms with nothing to do? Bottom line, we need more because, believe me, there are many more young people that will be in his situation real soon. Then what? It shouldn't be just the rich that can afford these programs that may help our young adults be a contributing part of society. After all, isn't that the goal?

MEDS

When Keith was around nine years old, he became very difficult to teach. When the teacher told me that he was "not available for learning," I knew I had to do something. We took him to the psychiatrist, who suggested he be put on medicine, Prozac, for the first time. I took in a sharp breath as if I was punched in the gut. I stared at the doctor, confused. "Why Prozac?" I asked. The doctor explained that they have found that it slows down the mind enough to receive new information. This was something we never wanted but felt as though we didn't have a choice if we wanted him to continue to learn, so we went with it. What the doctor was saying made sense, but the last thing we wanted was for Keith to be on meds that could possibly change his behavior, not to mention the possible side effects. As the doctor continued explaining things to us, I was kind of lost in the thought of our boy on meds. But what kind of mother would I be if I didn't help him continue to learn and calm his mind?

GROUND HOG DAY

My mind was reeling with what could happen as we left the doctor's office and headed to get the prescription filled. I was on autopilot as we filled the script and just stared at the bottle in my hand.

My husband and I talked about it the rest of the day, trying to sort out if this was the right thing for Keith or not. In the end, we decided to try it for our son's sake. It was about him, not us.

Prozac seemed to help for a while, and Keith was back to himself. We were glad and felt that we made the right choice at the time. After a couple years, when he was around eleven, it stopped working, so we went back to the doctor, and he changed it to Paxil, which seemed to work well except he was sleepy all the time. Teachers were complaining of him sleeping in class and outside waiting for class to start. We tried having him taking it at different times and everything, but it didn't change anything. He stayed on Paxil for a few years, and eventually he ran out one day and never told me, but we didn't notice a difference in him at all, so we didn't bother putting him back on it. I'm saying that if he needed it, we would have gone back to the doctor to talk about options.

Giving our kids meds is a sensitive subject for many families. If we never had to put Keith on meds, it would have been great, but he really needed something to help his mind slow down enough to learn. If you ever feel pressured to start meds or that you should take them off meds, make the decision with your child's best interest in mind. You know your child better than anyone, and you must do what is right for that child, and sometimes, that means giving them meds or taking them off meds. Either way, do what you know is right for the child. Don't feel bad for trying. Everyone's situation and child are different; make the choice that is right for your child.

After moving back to Seattle for a couple of years, we moved to El Paso, and it was there that Keith was bullied in an aggressive way for the first time. He was in middle school at this point. He went to the bathroom, and while in the stall, a kid from his class came in and began taunting him and banging/kicking on the door until it swung open and hit Keith in the head. Keith ran out of the bathroom to his class to tell the teacher, and the boy was removed from his class for good. Other than that, he really wasn't bullied much. At least, not that he told us about; he didn't always tell us.

He graduated from high school in Florida and continued to take programs after graduating, trying to get him ready for work and life. Although I truly am grateful for all the job training that had been afforded him, I do not feel like it has been enough, mainly because the world isn't ready for him or anyone like him. He is as ready as he can be, but it has taken years for him to find work. I do believe it's partially due to the application process online. This process may be easier for companies, but not for the applicants.

As if that wasn't enough, the social situational questions after the application are extremely difficult for anyone on the spectrum. It's unfair to the applicants, because they aren't even given the opportunity to show what they can do. If someone on the spectrum is totally honest on this part of the application, they will never get a chance because social situations are very difficult for them.

Keith is working now with a company that hires those with disabilities. We are happy for him because he may be able to move out like he wants to one day and is less likely to lose his job. But it's been a long and rough road to get him here, so be ready for it. Being autistic can be hard, but not always because of the child/adult all the time. The common thing that we hear and say is that a person on the spectrum doesn't handle change well, but "normal" people who don't take the time to be nice or understanding aren't willing to accept someone who is different, and that is not accepting change either. Society will not make it easy, but with so many people on the spectrum, they need to adjust to our kids as well as us teaching our kids to fit in to this world that belongs to everyone, not just those who are "normal."

OTHER PEOPLE

This brings up an issue that will be harder than anything and will be a continuous problem—society, other people, and their opinions, suggestions, looks, and stares. As your child gets older and it becomes more apparent that he/she are "different," You will begin to see the world in a new way, and that new way is not always in a good light.

Now let's be real, the first time you get that certain "look" from others, you will want to but can't beat up everyone who looks at your child, though you may feel like it at times! We are only human, and our natural instinct will be to protect our children. Every day and every reaction will be different depending upon your mood at the time. I have cursed people out, and I have just rolled my eyes and walked away, but just remember that your kids are watching you and how you handle situations. I think it bothers us more than our kids, so if you think about it, it is probably better to just let it go.

Some people think that they are being nice when you tell them that your child has autism and they say, "I'm sorry." I say, "I'm not. Our son is the best person I know!" I don't know what people are thinking. I would never say that to someone about their loved one.

Our need to protect our children is strong, and when that is challenged, we can go overboard. Strangers' stares, questions, or advice are really irrelevant to your life, so don't let it affect you. They don't know your life and what you go through every day. Let it go!

Okay, so we are obviously very involved parents and have tried and continue to try to find what's best for our son even though he is an adult. Being an adult doesn't change anything about his needs. Watching our son grow up in a world that is not always understanding of those who are different has not been easy. To an extent, it has improved. Watching the faces of people dealing with our son can be difficult, whether it be at a register or restaurant; even his doctor has given him a look the made me want to say something. This is obviously still an issue. Most of the public has now at least heard of autism but are not sure what it is or what it looks like. People still seem to think that there is a look or extreme behavior that would make autism more noticeable; this can be frustrating. I understand that unless someone is directly affected by something, they really do not get it, but this doesn't make it any less difficult to watch someone give him "that look." The one that says, "What's the matter with you?" When we were trying to find him a job and taking him to different places to apply, we were very aware of how people notice his awkwardness.

Although graduation is and was a momentous occasion, it's also a love-hate ball of emotion. Knowing that he will now have to face the cruel world that has little to nothing to offer someone with autism made it even scarier. Do not wait until your child is graduating high school to start your search for a program after school is over. Talk to people, look online for programs, get as much information as possible, and you still may find that you have to kind of settle for a second or third choice until you can get the one you want.

I believe it is just silly to think that our children can learn all they need to be an adult in life by then! Many young adults don't know what they want to do with their life at that age. How can we expect that our autistic adults will be ready for adulthood?

I am just a mom; I believe being a parent was all I've have ever been good at, and I think we have done great with our children. The problem is when you have a child that needs more from the world than you can give, life becomes extremely frustrating. Raising children is hard enough without having to depend on the state/government to help your child with the essentials to have a better life. I do understand that, within the umbrella of autism, there are many abilities and needs; I do not pretend that there are bigger issues than what our son requires, but when you are in it and live it every day, all you care about is what your child needs. I know that is true for most every parent.

One day, things will get better, and I hope someone reads this that can and will help all those touched by autism. I am doing what I can by trying to help the next family any way I can. That is my goal. I don't know how to help except to start a conversation and hope it goes somewhere.

Now, sometimes, you will have family members who are in denial or have all the answers. This is more difficult because they are family and you have to deal with them at times. Just let them know that your child's condition and how you handle him/her is not up for discussion. You can always leave if they continue to be pushy and opinionated. If you need someone to talk to outside family, the best thing is finding a support group where you feel comfortable. Yes, you may have to try a few to find the right fit, and don't feel bad about it. There are also online support groups, and that way, you don't even have to leave your house.

It is very important that you have an outlet so that you can be a better version of yourself for everyone involved. Even though you will try not to feel bad about getting some time to yourself, you need and deserve it. We all need that! I know that this sounds insane when your children are young and need you so much, but something has to give or the stress will drive yourself and your spouse insane. Unfortunately, the divorce rate is higher when you have a child with autism.

Find someone you trust to give you time together and date each other. If you tend to worry too much, go out after the child is asleep and have someone sit then.

Knowing this is easier said than done. Plan it. Set it as an alarm on your phone! Even if it's something small like a long soak in the tub together, get some of the intimacy back in your relationship. Or read a romance novel for ten minutes, draw, do something for a few minutes every day that has nothing to do with anything but you or something you and/or your spouse like to do! If you must adjust it, change or alter what it is or how long, that's fine, but do it whenever you can.

VISUAL LISTS

I mentioned visual list earlier; hopefully, you have some information on what it is and how to make and use one. These lists can make it so much easier after the initial start, because it's a change from what the child is doing now. I was able to get input from Keith to make him feel that he had some say in what was on the list. (Remember that those on the spectrum think very differently, so saying that I gave him some say didn't mean I let him make all the decisions.) I tried so hard to help our son that I already had a similar system in place before I knew there was a name for this list, so I just merged *the ideas together.*

Being on the spectrum is harder when they don't feel some amount of control. Besides, the parent is in control of the choices given. This way, you have more control overall. If you need help, ask! Sometimes the biggest challenge is you and your ability to ask for help. Granted, if my husband or daughter heard me talking about asking for help, it would be a long day. I'm not good at it!

The thing is, when it came to our son, I had no problems asking all kinds of questions because not knowing what to do for your child is an extremely helpless feeling! As the parents, we expect to be able to protect our children, and at times, you will feel as though you have failed them in some way, but as long as you don't give up and expect things from the child, you will not fail them! No one ever said that parenting was easy, no matter the child. Don't beat yourself up; keep doing what you can! As long as you keep working for them, they will keep working for you.

This reminds me of something that happened when Keith was little that taught me a lot. When Keith was about four years old, I told him that his birthday was coming. Now, at this time, his birthday was two weeks away. I went on cleaning the house, and after about ten minutes, I realized I didn't see him. I called him, went in his room, and started to panic because he wasn't anywhere in the house. I happened to go through the kitchen and saw him on the porch with his coat on, just sitting there. I went outside and asked him what he was doing, and he said he was waiting for his birthday to come.

It was at that moment I realized so much about how his mind worked. I grabbed the calendar and showed him when his birthday was, and every day, we would cross off the days until his birthday so that it was something he could understand. This changed everything. Not only did it start the list, but it gave us so much more insight to the way he thinks and sees things. It was so eye opening.

Visual lists can be a huge game changer in helping an autistic child understand the process of things, which can be extremely helpful for the parents. Because most children with autism have a difficult time with change, having a list with pictures and words eventually helps the child know what's coming up next.

Think about it, we all use things like calendars, cell phones, or agendas to help us plan our days, weeks, and years. A visual list for a child is the same thing. Though it should be more detailed to keep the child's attention, it serves the same purpose. Just as we use these techniques to prepare us for our day, this will help some children be more at ease because they will know what and when the next thing supposed to happen. It can help the child feel more at ease because they will know and understand what is expected of them.

Things that helped me were to realize that the way some autistic people see the world is extremely different than the way we do. If you can imagine feeling as though you are in a world that is totally and completely strange and scary and then having things expected of you, and you have no clue what to do or how to do it, this can be terrifying. Though it is hard to imagine your own child having to deal with this on a daily basis, it will help you learn how to teach them what they will need in life.

Please understand, I know that, in the beginning, it will be very trying and difficult for everyone, but in the end, it will help with even the smallest things. Lists can be made for brushing teeth, getting dressed, going to school, going to a friend or family's house, and doctor's visits. The possibilities are endless, and there is nothing like the satisfaction you get as a parent to watch your child grow and learn, knowing you have something to help them get through life a little easier.

We made a mourning list, after school list, dinner list, and a night-night list, and at the end of the week, if he did well, he had a small reward for working so hard. It is also very helpful to have mobile lists for situations outside the home that the child may need direction on such as restaurants. For Keith, we made them with index cards on a key ring and laminated them. We would review them before we even got out of the car so Keith was somewhat prepared. After some time, we didn't need them anymore.

This is an example of what an index card may look like (similar to what we did for Keith):

Going To A Restaurant

- First, someone will show us to a table. (This person doesn't take our order.)
- Second, the next person that comes to our table will take our drink order. (This is our waiter/waitress.)
- Third, that person will bring our drinks and then we can order our food.
- Fourth, we wait for our food to be cooked and then the waiter/waitress will bring our food to the table.
- Fifth, we all eat our food, and when we are all done eating, we will ask for the bill and pay the bill.
- Sixth, we can all leave

This is how our son's list looked so he knew what to expect. He had a habit of telling the first person he saw working there what he wanted to eat and drink. Then he would eat so fast and want to leave when we were still eating. Using these mobile lists made things go so much smoother when dealing with things outside the home but are necessary. I don't believe in just staying home because others got uncomfortable. This is the world Keith has to live in, and he needs to learn to get used to this world the best he can as early as he can, and the more others are exposed to people with different abilities, the better for us all.

The visual list you may use at home would look differently, because it would be on a large poster board or what I used, a trifold board that was put on the wall in Keith's room.

This is a list of things you may need to make a visual list:

- poster board
- markers
- stickers the child likes
- Velcro circles
- sheet protectors (I cut these in half to make pouches for the task achieved)
- laminate
- stapler
- pictures of actions expected of the child (you can find these online)

This will get everything started. I suggest, if it's possible, have him/her sit with you to help with ideas while making the list. Keith helped me a lot with ideas for what would work to help him remember things and what rewards he would like. I drew his pictures, laminated them, and put them on the board with Velcro so he could remove and reuse them.

Here is an example of what Keith's morning list looked like:

- wake up
- take off night-night clothes
- put on shirt
- put on pants
- put on socks
- put on shoes
- go to bathroom

- get toothbrush
- put toothpaste on toothbrush
- brush teeth
- rinse mouth
- rinse toothbrush
- put toothbrush back
- go to kitchen
- eat breakfast
- get on bus and go to school

Now this may seem like a lot, but if you can understand that they learn differently and that everything is foreign to them, making their list will come much easier. It must be done step by step, and as they get older, the list will be much less detailed.

As he/she does each action, they come back to the board and remove that action and put in the "done" pouch. This way, they will know what comes next and feel more in control. This is the way the list works. The in-between time is time for them to do whatever they want so they can recover from the demands of the day. A person on the spectrum needs some down time because things can become overwhelming. It takes an extreme amount of energy to follow directions, be corrected, and try to do what is asked of them all day. So it is very important that they are allowed down time to do what they want to do. We all need to recharge at times, but for someone on the spectrum, it is imperative that this time is allowed every day to center themselves.

Of course, I didn't always know how to teach Keith how to do things or reach him, but things happened that I paid attention to that gave me clues on how he may think. For example, I was having a stressful time one day and told him to clean his room. I came back after some time to check on him, and the room hadn't changed, and he was still playing, I became angry and began to throw things in boxes to take out of his room. He began to cry, saying that those were his friends, and I felt like crap.

I couldn't stop thinking about what happened that day and how I could have handled things differently. I realized that maybe he did not understand at all what "clean your room" meant. The more I thought about it, of course he didn't! My guilt consumed me until the next day, when I could try to recover from the way I must have made him feel. I spoke with Keith the best way I could, and we ended up cleaning his room together, but I had to show him exactly what "clean your room" meant. Put all your cars in this bucket, put all your blocks in this bucket, and so on. But because I try to always stick to what I say, the toys I did put in a box, he had to earn them back by keeping his room clean, which he did with no problem. This was very hard, but after that, I never had to worry about his room being messy again. I know that I overreacted, but it ended up teaching him well; the thing about it was he recovered faster than I did.

CHANGES

During your research on autism, you will see that one of the main things that the kids have a hard time with is change. It can be anything from small changes such as putting on a different shirt to going to a new school or even moving to a new home. All these things can cause a lot of stress for the child and the parents if the child is not prepared. Of course, this is life, and we all know that things can happen last minute, and we may have no control over it; therefore, having some things in place for these occasions is extremely helpful.

The best place to start is with regular things that happen in your family every day. The visual list that we just shared usually helps the child feel comfortable because they know what is going to happen next.

Basically, a visual list can give a step-by-step guide to many things the child may need to learn, and because of this, there is less stress and/or tantrums. Try putting yourself in the place of your child. If you were put in a situation that terrified you and you had no clue what was going to happen next, you would freak out too. During my son's life, I have always tried to see things through his eyes. This gave me a greater insight into him and how he thinks, which has allowed me to teach him more easily over the years. Granted, some things may have been harder than others, but eventually, he would just figure it out or something would happen that gave me a clue as to how to help him understand better.

To give a little background, my husband was in the army for twenty years, and that meant we had a lot of moving, packing, traveling, schools, teachers, doctors, houses, rooms, therapists; I could go on and on, but needless to say, our son has had to get used to change early on and often. I feel that we have had a lot of practice preparing Keith for changes in life.

One of the best things we did was to regularly talk about the change that was coming, mark it on a calendar, and count down the days with Keith and, if possible, show pictures of the new school or house, even the new teacher if we could get it. Teachers usually understand how a smooth transition can make it easier for everyone. This can also get them ready for appointments they don't particularly care for like doctors, the dentist, and other necessary things in life. I was a hairstylist, and once a year, we had a cut-a-thon for autism where I acquired a few children with autism as clients. This led me to analyzing the necessities of life. I found that most mothers would attempt to cut the child's hair themselves rather than try to go through the stress of asking some stranger who may not understand the situation.

After giving this a lot of thought, preparing the child for this appointment and other necessities like dentists and doctors can be done with less tears. Learning the need for reassurance and routine will help. Begin by first telling the child about the need for the appointment and that everyone does it, even Mom and Dad. Speak to the stylist, dentist, or doctor about bringing the child in just to begin to become accustomed to the office or salon. During the visits, always talk to them about what will happen, why and, if possible, have the child meet the person they will see at the appointment.

After some time, the child will become less and less stressed out about the event, and then let the child know that the day will come that they will have something done at that place. If there is another sibling, allow the child to watch them go first and explain everything as it happens. This will give you even more tools to help the child such as a mobile visual list on index cards that can be reviewed right in the car before the appointment or right in the waiting room.

This may seem like a lot, but when the child begins to deal with changes and such better, there is nothing like the pride you will feel that you gave your child the tools to get through some of those necessary appointments or changes. As time goes on, dealing with change will be as simple as a conversation and reminders of past situations that they made it through.

I do understand that autism is a huge umbrella that ranges all over, but I beg you, please know that with some patience and time, any child can improve in even the smallest of ways. Keep your eyes open for opportunities to learn from them so you can more easily teach them. Use things they like or that they obsess over to help get/keep their attention. Those with autism are an open book; we just have to learn to read their book by watching and being open to how they see the world.

APPOINTMENTS

When our kids were young, we were told by the dentist that it would benefit both our kids to have sealants put on their teeth because we knew they didn't brush their teeth very well. We agreed and set the appointment. I was hoping that all would go well. Keith had done well with a simple checkup, so I was hoping for the best. We had kind of started having Denyse go first so that Keith watch to see what would be happening to him when it was his turn, and it usually worked out well, so I wasn't too worried.

The day came for the dentist appointment and I tried to prepare Keith for what was about to happen, and he seemed okay. Even after explaining this to the staff, they took our daughter while I was taking Keith to the bathroom with me because we both needed to go. I was very upset and tried to explain, yet again, the situation, but the dentist wouldn't allow Keith to watch Denyse have her teeth done. Though I was angry, I didn't want to upset Keith, so I tried to let it go.

After a short time, Denyse came out, and it was Keith's turn, I stayed calm and talked to him the whole time. He got in the chair and laid back. As soon as he did, the staff began treating him as though he was already being difficult which, in turn, caused him to react. The dentist immediately put a thing in his mouth that held his mouth open, and by this time, Keith was crying and thrashing about. The doctor said that he would have to put him in a papoose. I didn't know what it was until they explained it to me, and I was completely against it. I told them that no one is tying down my son. I said that I would hold Keith down and "you do what you have to do." At that point, I straddled my son in the chair to hold him down and held down his arms while sitting on his legs. In this position, I'm looking him right in the face and watching him struggle against me and the dentist. I wanted to cry so badly but didn't want him to see me upset.

This was very traumatic for the both of us. When it was over, I was shaking and holding back tears as we walked to the car. I kept apologizing to Keith over and over again, I felt awful for what I did. He would say that it was okay, but I couldn't stop apologizing until we were in the car and putting on our seatbelts. I said that I was sorry again, and Keith said, "Are we still talking about this, Mom?" Denyse and I laughed as we drove off. He had gotten over it faster than I did.

We realized after that day that he does, at times, get over things faster than we do. Of course, it depends on what is going on at the time, but he is much stronger than we think. We learned that we can't assume that our children will react as we would to any given situation.

SOCIALIZATION

Keith still has issues with socializing. This will probably be something that he will always struggle with, because having autism really makes it difficult to understand what others are thinking or feeling at times. Not to say that he can't or won't improve, but it may always be an issue. The problem with socializing is other people and how they will respond to him. Autism comes with some common quirks such as being socially awkward. This can be noticeable, and sometimes, it's a little more subtle.

As a child, a person with autism might play beside other children instead of with them, which is referred to as parallel play, or the child may find a place all to themselves. Many prefer to be alone most of the time, and some find social situations extremely uncomfortable all together.

While the child is young, it is extremely important to socialize them as often as possible. This can be very difficult not only for the child but for the parents/whole family. We found that, over the years, although there were many meetings and conversations about socialization with the school for Keith, nothing ever came of it. The schools would brush it off and state that he "gets it" throughout the day during school. Well, if anyone knows anything about autism at all, they would know that they don't "just get" anything or they wouldn't be considered autistic. What I mean to say is "typical" children learn and or pick up manners and behaviors from those around them as time goes on. A child with autism is usually not very attentive to his/her surroundings to pick up or learn many behaviors. Most of what an autistic child learns is from many hours of teaching and repetition. Still, the autistic person may always be somewhat socially awkward, and that's not a bad thing; it's part of who they are as a person.

Now that Keith is an adult, I wish the schools had done more to help him socially. I believe that just as there is therapy for speech, occupational, and physical, there should be a sort of social therapy. If starting with all the other therapies as young as possible is important, so should social therapy be applied early on.

We live in an extremely social world, and if someone is different, it is obvious and puts others off. Having a disability is hard enough, whether it's physical or otherwise; the world has a very difficult time having the patience or time to understand it unless it is someone in their family. Believe it or not, I get it to an extent, but I could never be mean or hateful to someone I don't even know no matter what.

If you have a child with autism, please fight for as much assisted socialization as possible; that is your right and your child's right. Teach your child all that you can and learn all that you can about ways to socialize. Yes, it will be hard for the parent and the child, but please believe it will be worth all the tears in the end.

Keith, as an adult, carries himself in a way that says, "Don't talk to me," so he doesn't get approached very often, and that is probably why. We have spied on him walking around the mall to see what he does on his own, and he needs more work on walking around people, or if someone talks to him, he doesn't notice, so they are ignored. I don't think that he expects a stranger to talk to him. It's almost like he doesn't really see people in a sense; they are just things to get around to get where he wants to go.

When he has to engage with someone at a register or to ask for something, he does pretty well. Sometimes, he will talk too fast or run his words together and kind of gets frustrated when he has to repeat himself. I can understand his frustration to a point because he has always been corrected in his young life, and I'm sure it gets old.

I recall an episode that happened with my husband and Keith at a gas station. They went in for some snacks, and a guy was standing with the door open to the soda that Keith wanted, so he just walked up in front of the guy and grabbed his drink. Now, of course, the guy had something to say, and he and my husband had a few words, but nothing aggressive. You always feel the need to protect your child even if they are wrong. My husband apologized but let the guy know that he should be careful what he says to people even if they are rude. Needless to say, Keith and my husband talked about what happened and how he should handle that situation next time.

Dealing with the public is hard, because you have to use the opportunity to teach your child and try to deal with the other person at the same time. I believe that bad behavior should always be corrected, no matter how hard it can be at times. The other person, on the other hand, may be more difficult. Don't expect others to be understanding all the time, because you will be disappointed.

We have had many encounters with others being insensitive and many very nice people. People are going through their own stuff and carry it over to others that don't deserve it.

I know this to be true, because Keith has experienced this and told us about it in his own way. We were at the mall, and Keith was at a store trying to buy something with his card, and something was going wrong with it, so he called my husband, and he got it straightened out. While walking back through the mall, Keith asked if people thought he was crazy. I wanted to lose it, but we asked him if anyone said anything to him at that store, and he said no. He could tell by the guy's face at the register that he was looking at him differently or that he was just aggravated that he had to take extra time to help Keith.

It's like it takes people by surprise that he is different somehow, and they look at him like something is wrong with him. It's very hard to know that people look at him like that all the time, but we can't do much about it but use it to educate others as much as possible and prepare our kids for the world we live in because it's their world too.

The stories you hear about other children with autism that are very successful but may have started out having hard time dealing with being autistic, I always wonder how they got there. What happened that closed that gap for them, and how can I figure it out for our son? Keith has goals and dreams, what is the secret? I know the answer but would rather dream that there is a secret. But the truth is that it goes back to the fact that everyone with autism is not the same and their path will be different as well. Who they become is a mystery, as with any child, but we can do our best to help them along the way.

LISTENING AND PAYING ATTENTION

Most people look at you when you are talking to let you know that they are listening. Parents with children on the spectrum know that this can be a problem with their child. For Keith, we noticed this pretty early on. It really got our attention how much of a problem it was during his testing. The doctor kept trying to get Keith to look at him, and he couldn't.

Earlier, I touched on reading books about autism that may or may not relate to your child, in saying that, I did read a book that shed light on an issue with those on the spectrum. Though the book scared me at first because of the life the person had in an institution. It did surprise me that this book taught me something that was very interesting about our son. I guess you can find answers in unexpected places.

While reading about this man's life, he addresses looking people in the eye. The man was unable to do so because, as he explains, it was "physically painful." He couldn't really explain it more than that. That moment made me pause and think of Keith. I wondered what it was like for him. I let the thought go and continued reading the book, but a few days afterward, I was talking to him, and as usual, he wasn't looking at me. I blurted out the question, "Boy, why don't you look at me when you talk to me?" (Boy is an affectionate term in many Spanish families.)

Keith's answer, "Because it hurts."

I just stared at him in shock. I really didn't know what to expect, but since that day, I never asked him to look at me again. If he was expected to for some reason, I told him to try looking at the person's hair or chin to be respectful. Do I believe this to be true for everyone? No, I'm sure that it is different for each child. Gaining that information from Keith was huge for me. Any time I learned something related to our son was exciting and interesting.

Today, when Keith speaks to someone, he looks deep into their eyes with his dark chocolate eyes, and they know that he is listening. This also made me think about Manny and how he would "watch" TV—sitting beside it or sitting sideways so that the TV was a side view. He rarely watched TV facing it, but that didn't mean that he wasn't paying attention or listening to what was going on in the show or movie. Our way of thinking is that you face the person that you are interacting with, but in the mind of a person with autism, you don't have to even look as though you are paying any attention at all to know exactly what is going on around you if you want to. I understand that this may be a little confusing, because I stated earlier that many on the spectrum don't just learn things because of what is going on around them. Though this is true for many, the child does hear and is listening when you may not think so. A person may not know what to do with the information of what they hear, but they are listening.

When working with your child, it is helpful to use short sentences and to not overexplain or repeat yourself. To this day, Keith gets annoyed when he is asked too many questions or the same question to many times. I think it has to do with processing the information and knowing what to do with it. I wish I could explain it more than that. For him, short and sweet is the best way that I have found to speak with Keith to get the response I'm looking for, otherwise, he gets frustrated and overwhelmed.

I GOT TOO EXCITED

Yet again, Keith opens my eyes. As I have probably stated before, he continues to teach us about who he is and how he learns. Keith has been showing us a more engaging, social side of him that we have not really seen. I truly believe that everything happens for a reason, and although we may not know or understand the reasoning at the time, it works out for the best in the end.

As parents, we carry our children's struggles more than their accomplishments, but it can make things very difficult at times. There was a time we thought Keith was going to go to one of these college programs and wanted him to focus on school more, so we thought it was a sound decision for him to quit his job a few weeks before he was supposed to start. Turns out, we really could not afford the program at this college. He had no job and no school! You can imagine our frustration and guilt! It seemed we had made all kinds of mistakes in this situation and allowed our excitement to take over.

Keith didn't work for about three years and was not very happy about sitting in his room. Now, understand, this is the same child who usually wanted to just be in his room and focus on his movie ideas. He thought he could just go make a movie and be rich—that easy. We have had many very honest conversations about how difficult it is to be another Steven Spielberg. I say all this because, now, he seems to have more of an understanding about how life works; now, he just wants a job while he works on his movie ideas. I knew that it would take time, but even after all his twenty-one years (at the time), I still get so consumed with his current thinking or behavior that I forget that the day usually comes when he just gets it!

It is normal to get a little caught up sometimes, but it's okay; they will show you when they got it, and no matter the age, the thrill of their accomplishments are always just as exciting! We are all learning our way through life; we should enjoy the education with our children. No one's life is meant to be like anyone else's, so enjoy the life you have; you may stumble, you may even fall, but as long as you don't give up, your child won't either!

BALANCING YOUR MIND

Balancing life is hard, but life as a parent is much more difficult. The mind of a parent is on overdrive most of the time because we are always thinking of what needs to be done or should have been done for our children. It's a cycle that is ongoing. I brought mine to a whole new level at one point in Keith's life that probably was a waste of energy, but I was just trying to get into his mind a little more.

I believe it was when Keith was a preteen that I began this way of thinking. I thought that there was a separation between Keith and autism. How much of his behavior was him just being a kid and how much of it was autism? Looking back on this now, I realize that I was reaching for something that didn't exist. I even asked his doctor at one point, and he looked at me as though he never had that question asked before. The doctor suggested that I was doing a great job with him and obviously knew Keith very well and that I should just continue on with what I was doing with him. At the time, I still thought there was something to what I thought, but after years of raising him, I came to the realization that I was putting extra stress and pressure on myself that was unnecessary.

Sometimes, when you get a thought in your mind that you think may help you understand your child, you can't stop it from pushing an issue that really doesn't have a resolution. You just want to help your child as much as possible. What people outside of this world don't realize is that it is a heavy thing to carry knowing that most of what happens for your child is up to you. It feels so unfair to you and your child because you don't feel qualified for this position. Overwhelming is a complete understatement.

As parents, when we are about to have a child, it can be nerve-racking to think of being responsible for someone else's life, but having a child with special needs is a whole new level of responsibility. This is why we need as much help as possible. Don't be afraid to ask for help at any point in your child's life, because we don't have all the answers. Hopefully, you are able to create a community of resources around yourself to be there for you at any time. I know that this isn't easy, but it will be worth the effort for your family in the long run. You are not alone in all that you experience in life no matter what it is. If you ever feel that way, push it away because it is not true. We all feel this at times, but do not continue with this way of thinking; it will only keep the negative thoughts going and will not help anyone.

KEITH ALWAYS MAKES US LAUGH

Our son has made us laugh more than anything and continues to do so. It makes it all worth it. He does not like when someone is mad or sad even if, at the time, we are trying to teach him something such as trying to get him to relax enough to fall asleep. This is just one of many stories that I will never forget.

When Keith was about ten years old, he still had trouble falling asleep well at night, and this was causing him to sleep in school. At the time, he was seeing a psychologist (only because we had to in order to get his meds at the time). Now this doctor was…let me find the right word…an idiot who must have found his license in a cereal box. That being said, he asked if we believe in spanking; we said yes. At this point, my husband and I looked at each other wondering what that had to do with getting our son to sleep better.

Well, this genius said that we should *put* him in a sleeping position and if he moved at all, spank him every time! Now, I don't know about you, but that would not make me relax and fall asleep or even want to go to bed for fear of getting smacked! Needless to say, we never went back.

It was shocking to think that this man really gave advice like this to people, not to mention the thought that someone may actually do it! We just couldn't believe it! The only thing we took from that was to let him get comfortable, pick a sleeping position, and explain that when he goes to bed, it wasn't time to play; it was time to relax and go to sleep.

After a few nights of talking him through this to see if it would sink in, our son looked at my husband (who was taking his turn trying to get him to sleep) and looked at me in the doorway of his room and said, "Dad, haven't we done this before?" We lost it at that point and laughed so hard that our son looked at us like he didn't know what was so funny.

He is the best. Every time I think of that moment, I cannot help but to laugh at the whole situation. After that, we decided to relax him the best we could so that he could sleep. Even though we all know that hitting a child always makes kids relax to fall asleep, we just couldn't do it.

There will be plenty of times when you will receive advice that is unwanted or that just won't work for your child. Everyone has advice, especially those without children at all or those who have children that are "normal." It is crazy the things that people are willing to say, and much of it is hurtful or just plain mean.

Since our son Keith was little, we did, as I said earlier, get many opinions from people that were unwarranted and hurtful. At the time, I was mostly unsure how to deal with it other than walking away and crying my eyes out!

Around the time we first got the diagnosis, I overheard a woman that was a customer at the salon I worked at say that if she was pregnant and knew the baby had autism, she would get an abortion. I froze, looked at the coworker that was doing her hair, bit my lip, and rushed to the bathroom. I was a mess and had to go home; I cried the rest of the day. People can be so hurtful.

Having a child with autism can be extremely hard to the point that you have no words for what you're feeling, but it's okay because tomorrow will still come, and you will still get up and get the day going whether you know what's coming next or not. Having a child with any disability can be difficult at times, but so can most children; they still need your love unconditionally, they need your understanding, and they need all that you can give them. They deserve that.

WHEN KEITH IS SICK

When you first have a child, you learn rather early on that the doctors depend on you, the parent, to answer all the questions about your child. At first, it is a scary experience. What if you don't know, or what if you forget to tell the doctor something important? After some time, you do learn to "read" your child and their behavior.

What I have learned through Keith's life is that this is going to still be the case today. Keith doesn't let me know when he is feeling sick very often; I just notice when something isn't quite right or he has been coughing. My mom radar goes on alert to any changes in him. Not that I am weirdly high strung or anything; I just know him. What I do know is that he has a high pain tolerance and is prone to bronchitis.

When taking him to the doctor, he looks to me to answer any questions asked. I have tried to explain many times that he is the only one who knows what he is feeling, but I do believe that, at least for Keith, this is a very difficult thing for him to do. When I watch him answer questions about other things, it's not a problem, but when asking questions about how he feels physically, he really struggles and makes a face of anguish. This pains me, and I feel helpless because I don't know what he is feeling. Yes, I am one of the only people who can get answers from him about certain things, but it takes time and many questions asked in different ways. But in a medical setting, it becomes stressful because you want him to get the help he needs.

Only recently did I learn that this inability Keith had to express his emotions or feeling had a name. Meriam-webster medical definition of Alexithymia is the inability to identify and describe one's feelings.

Recently, Keith took himself to the emergency room and didn't tell anyone. I was out of town, and he and our daughter Denyse were staying at the house. Denyse was at work at the time. I received a phone call from the ER doctor that she had Keith there and he was having a hard time answering medical history and other questions. After I removed my heart from my throat, I gave her his medical history and helped answer any other questions she needed. I also asked her to have him call me. I was terrified. What could be happening to him that he felt the need to go to the ER? The doctor I spoke with was calm and explained that he was complaining of chest pain. I was freaking out but held it together until I spoke with Keith. I couldn't wait for him to call me, so I called him.

Keith said that his chest hurt, and the night before, he felt like his heart was racing. I told him that he would be okay and that Denyse would be there as soon as school was over. Because he had chest pain, they wanted to keep him overnight, and he has never had to stay in the hospital before, so by the time my daughter got there, the nurse told her that Keith said he wanted to leave. She told him that he had to stay and that she would stay with him, but she had to pick up her son and get a sitter for him. I asked Denyse to be sure to bring his pillow and blanket so he would be more comfortable. What Denyse and I couldn't understand or expect was that Keith would resort to something he mostly did as a kid—echolalia. As an adult, it showed as a phrase he heard recently and began saying it to the nurses as they came in and asked him about why he came to the ER. As you know, if you spend any time in the hospital, every person that comes in your room asks you a lot of questions. He would say, "I just wanted to make sure that everything was on the up and up." When they asked him why he came to the ER, though he made the answer fit the question, it wasn't the best answer to give. Keith does not do well with a lot of questions, especially repeated ones, I think, most especially, questions about how he feels. I wish I knew why this is so difficult for him. All I can do is try to help him as best I can.

After the nurse would leave the room, Denyse spoke with him about really answering the questions, and if he needed help, she would help, but he had to let her know how he felt. Because Keith became stressed about staying in the hospital and wasn't sure what was happening physically, and with so many questions being asked, he became frustrated and just used this phrase. I felt horrible for not being there for him in such a stressful situation. I wish I could have come through the phone to be there for him.

The result from all of this is that he has been struggling with anxiety. He has not been sleeping much because he can't stop thinking of all the negative things that have happened in his life as an adult. I think people outside of this world of autism really do not get the impact the world can have on our kids. I did beat myself up about this and how I could not have known something was wrong, but Keith obviously didn't know how to explain what he was feeling.

I am glad that he took himself to the ER, and we know what is going on, and it's not his heart. This also let me know that there is something else I need to teach him as far as handling himself in a medical situation. Somehow, I will find a way to help him better handle it if and when he has to go to the doctor again. I know that I will make index cards for him with all his medical history and his doctors' information on it. That is a start, anyway.

Obviously, things will happen that remind you that you cannot possibly prepare your child for everything in life. This situation seems so obvious that I should have better prepared him for this. All we can do as parents is help them as best we can and add to their "list of life". Life is tricky and hard. The future is a mystery to us all. Do what you can to help your child and don't give yourself to hard of a time if you miss something.

I didn't think about the fact that, in this situation, I would have to have the conversation about letting people know that he has autism. It just took me back to a time the word bothered me, but there was also a time when this bothered Keith as well. Around the age of nine to high school age, Keith really didn't like being referred to as autistic in any way, and through these years, I would ask him why it bothered him so much. He would just say it did but didn't know why. Maybe he just didn't want to be different, and I could understand that.

Keith always seemed to have not let anything bother him like that, so it surprised us that it did. But as time passed, he realized it was not a big deal, so it doesn't bother him anymore. I bring this up because I do realize that this does bother many others, especially those who have Asperger's. My nephew who has Asperger's really gets upset and wants nothing to do with anything that has to do with autism, much less be referred to as having autism. What I feel he doesn't realize is that he is successful in his life because he has Asperger's. He graduated from high school with college credits and at the top of his class. He also was student body president and prom king. He has accomplished more than most because of who he is. Who knows who he would be with one piece missing from what makes him him.

If your child doesn't like being referred to as autistic, that's okay, but I don't believe it would last forever, so I wouldn't worry too much. At some point, the child may have heard something negative about it or even has seen others being treated differently by other children and doesn't want that to happen to them. Keeping open communication with your child is always the best way to help him or her to know how they feel about what is going on in their lives.

MOVING ON AFTER HIGH SCHOOL

There comes a time in every child's life when they move on from home to school or work. When you have a child with autism, it's not that simple. There are not that many options for our children with autism once they are out of the school system, and the good ones are extremely expensive. Not only does the price of a good program make a parent cringe, but there are only private loans to turn to. There will be no financial assistance because it is a non-degree program.

Something has got to change for adults with autism beyond high school! There has got to be more options out there for these people. Some of these young adults have goals and dreams just like anyone else. Our son wants to be a voice actor. Though we know that most people have a hard time making that dream job come true, it doesn't mean we stop trying to give people the chance that we would give to any other young adults.

Actually, if anyone knows anything about those with autism, it is their willingness to work, not waste time, be on time, and be dependable. Most autistic people would probably make the best employees.

Programs have got to be offered to these young adults once out of high school. More programs should be offered during high school, at a younger stage in the child's life to help the child learn and grow in more than just education but for possible future employment.

More and more children are diagnosed every day; some even going undiagnosed for many years. These children will grow to be adults who can do more than sweep a floor or clean up after someone. Being grateful for what is out there shouldn't mean settling for something that isn't beneficial or financially available for as many people as possible.

Many parents have struggled for everything their child has needed throughout the child's young life, and the bigger struggle starts after the age of twenty-one to twenty-two. The search for programs is one thing, but affording them is altogether a different animal. The thrill of finding what seems to be a dream program is quickly drowned out by the cost and/or location. The age limit also makes no sense because those who need to have more time to learn things will miss out. This is not a helpful system. If there were a program or system that would truly help the transition of these young adults to adulthood, it should start at the beginning of high school to give the child a chance to grow and learn what they need to know to have some skills to help them get a job. These young years go by fast, and the earlier we can teach them something helpful, the better chance they may have to get them started as an adult.

Until something changes in this country, we will continue to have one in every sixty-four adults with autism that will be graduating every year and have very limited options once out of high school. What will happen with these young people if they have nothing available to them? Be forgotten about in their homes until the caregiver is gone? Be put in a facility when this person is capable of holding a job? Either way, the state will be assisting in their life financially, so why not use the money at the right time for the right reason!

When you have kids, you always feel like their parent, no matter the age of your children. From the moment they are born, you feel responsible for not only their safety but also for their happiness. A child has a different way of seeing the world up until they grow and have some experiences that change their perspective. So how do you parent them in a way that will guide and protect them without being too overprotective? In order to learn, we all have to go through things to really understand the way things work in the world. Slowly but surely, parents try teaching their child all they can, the best they know how.

Think about your childhood; if you had siblings and you think of them today, did they get the same things from your upbringing that you did? Most likely, they didn't. The thing is, everyone is different and gets something different from every experience in life. That will include your children.

The things we realize as our children are growing up is very different from what is actually realized after they have grown. The reality is that we too are growing and learning right along with them. Life is constantly a learning process for everyone. The children, the parents, the family. We all have a role in each other's lives whether we want to or not. It's what we take from our experiences and how we handle them that makes us who we are and what we grow into.

Parenting is the best and hardest thing anyone can do in life. There is no greater gift than having a child, but there are no instructions. Loving and wanting the best for your children will lead the way.

ADULTHOOD

Keith has dreams; he wants to live on his own and be a voice actor. Right now, he wants to have his own apartment, and I'm not too worried about him being able to take care of himself within the home, because we have taught him as much as we could about caring for himself. He can cook, clean, wash clothes, and do the dishes and everything else it takes to live on his own.

The hard part is getting Keith to completely understand the financial part of living on his own—paying rent, utilities, and such. He needs to understand how much he needs to make for this to happen. Sometimes, I wish he could understand it better. You know how it goes; kids sometimes listen to others better than their parents. We attempt to help him understand, but I know one day he will get it, because he usually does.

Don't get me wrong, this will be a difficult time for me when he does move out, but it needs to happen. We need to know that he can care for himself; as parents, that is our job.

Other than how he can care for himself, he also is very independent in that on his days off, he rides his bike anywhere he wants to go. He also knows how to take the city bus. We are proud of all that he has accomplished, and we know that he will continue to grow as a person.

We now know that Keith may need to revisit some rules about life as he grows, because things change as you grow and the way you deal with them should. Life is change, and because this is usually an issue for those on the spectrum, we must find ways to help them adjust to it as best we can.

THE PERSON KEITH IS TODAY

Keith is very independent, and we couldn't be prouder of the person he has become. He is all the things we taught our kids to be—respectful, hard worker, nice, and happy. We know that his life isn't everything he wants it to be at the time, but we know that if he keeps working hard at it, he will get the career he is working for.

Keith is also a very pure person who doesn't seem to become tainted by the world in the way that many of us do. He also doesn't like for anyone to be sad or mad. When he apologizes, he means it. We teach our kids many things in life, but we all know that, in time, something will change the way they view life because of an experience we couldn't save them from. Though Keith has had some negative things happen in his life, some more than others, it still hasn't dulled his light. He is raw, open, genuine, caring, loving, and so much more. It can be scary to know this about your child, because we understand the world a little better, but overall, it is truly amazing to witness. Most think of an autistic person as someone in their own world, and that may be true, but I would rather be a part of that world of innocence at times than the reality of this world. As parents of these beautiful children, we have the ability to have one foot in the child's world and one foot in ours to find out how to help them succeed and learn all they can. It is an advantage for us and our children.

Keith has a job that he gets himself up for, walks to the city bus stop, and takes the bus forty-five minutes one way and back home. There was a time that Keith compared his life to his sister's, and it was so hard to explain the difference to him. He believed that he should do things in life when Denyse did, and it just didn't work out that way when he wanted to drive. He thought for a long time that he would one day drive, but that day never came. I remember he came to my husband and I out of the blue and said that he probably would not drive but he wanted to get a bike, something he never learned to do because he was scared that he would fall. Keith now has a three-wheel bike, and we now live in an area that he can get to many stores and the mall to on a bike. He loves his independence and doesn't want to lose that.

Keith does have hopes and dreams of being a voice actor, and we all know how hard that can be for anyone. I do believe that this will be harder for him as we have found his adult life to be to this point, but we will continue to help him pursue it anyway. We think that he can accomplish this dream as long as he doesn't give up and keeps training.

I have to admit that the battles with myself over certain things in his life have been a difficult reality at times. Like having to get over the "label" thing, I had to get over the fact that most jobs available are cleaning up after people, and being that he is currently a janitor, we all had to get over ourselves. A least he is working rather than sitting in his room upset that he isn't. He is also being paid well, and it's more than any mall job he could get near our house.

Trying to get Keith to understand how things work as an adult in life is an ongoing conversation. Because he wants to have his own place one day, we tell him that he could better afford it if he would work more than three days a week, but he doesn't want to. Truth is, he really doesn't like his job but is glad to have his own money, something I suppose we all have to learn at some point, and he is learning it now. Being that we are very straightforward with our kids, we always try to get him to understand all that we can. He probably doesn't want to move out right now anyway.

In case you are wondering what Keith's official and most recent diagnosis is, it's Asperger's. With an IQ of 86. When he was first diagnosed, the doctor said classic autism with an IQ of 64. We were told many times that IQs do not change, and that may be true, but if, at the time, the child doesn't know what is expected of them, how can you get an accurate number. I believe that sometimes it can change because the child may grow and change in time. I think this is what happened with Keith.

Obviously, much has changed and improved for Keith. Some things came easy, and some were not so easy, but as long as he keeps moving forward, so will we. I admire his determination; many of us would have given up on many things by now, but not him. That is not to say that he doesn't get frustrated at not getting a voice acting job, but he keeps trying. There are many traits of autism that we focus on and some, I believe, we can learn from that are very positive.

Keith still has things he can work on, mostly social things, but I still wait for the day when he will just get it. That is how he is, but if he doesn't, that's okay too, because he has already been successful in his life considering where he started. Social situations will probably always be a bit of a struggle for him, but I have faith in him and what he can accomplish, even one day having a true shot at his dream of voice acting. He even has a YouTube channel and has made business cards all by himself to pass out to people.

Keith is truly amazing, and we couldn't be prouder of the person he has grown to be. People do not think about what a person with autism must go through to "fit in" to this world—a lifetime of being corrected on almost everything. It must get old to have someone correcting what you do all the time. Most of us wouldn't put up with that for too long much less all day, every day. The strength he must have is unreal. Keith may read and write at about a fourth-grade level, but he has the heart of a warrior. No matter how many times he has been knocked down, he gets back up!

Keith, we can't wait to see the next chapter of your wonderful life, because you are an inspiring story!

ABOUT THE AUTHOR

Nydia Caraman was born the youngest of twelve children. Being one of many, she learned early on that family is one of the most important things in life. Watching her parents work hard to provide and care for her and her siblings made a huge impact on her, for she knew that one day, she too would take great care of her husband and children. Marrying and bearing two children young, she began the journey as the mother and wife she wanted to be. Little did she know how much she would learn.

First and foremost, being a wife, a mother, and a grandmother are the most important parts of her life. She has always craved an outlet for her creativity. It began with a passion for photography, grew into a career as a hairstylist, and finally has landed her here, writing this book. Throughout this journey of creating, her family has been constantly learning and experiencing the world in a light that most people don't get to. Sharing their lives and what they have learned about autism with you is exciting because their goal has always been to help others live life seeing it in the same light as they have.

CPSIA information can be obtained
at www.ICGtesting.com
Printed in the USA
BVHW030106160121
597838BV00004B/19

9 781644 684238